United States
Department of
Agriculture

Forest Service

Southern
Research Station

Resource Bulletin
SRS–169

Estimates of Biomass in Logging Residue and Standing Residual Inventory Following Tree-Harvest Activity on Timberland Acres in the Southern Region

Roger C. Conner and Tony G. Johnson

I0435087

The Authors:

Roger C. Conner, Research Forester, U.S. Forest Service,
Southern Research Station, Knoxville, TN 37919; and
Tony G. Johnson, Resource Analyst, U.S. Forest Service,
Southern Research Station, Asheville, NC 28804.

Front cover:
Logger in upland hardwoods in Arkansas. (photo by Tony G. Johnson)

January 2011

Southern Research Station
200 W.T. Weaver Blvd.
Asheville, NC 28804

Contents

Page

Introduction... 1

Biomass as Defined by FIA... 1

   Logging Residue.. 1

   Residual Inventory... 2

Types of Cutting... 2

Survey Years... 2

Results.. 3

Summary.. 4

Literature Cited... 4

Appendix... 5

   Index of Tables.. 7

   Tables A.1–A.26[a]... 9

[a] All tables in this report are available in Microsoft® Excel workbook files. Upon request, these files will be supplied in the format the customer requests. The use of trade or firm names in this publication is for reader information and does not imply endorsement by the U.S. Department of Agriculture of any product or service.

.

Estimates of Biomass in Logging Residue and Standing Residual Inventory Following Tree-Harvest Activity on Timberland Acres in the Southern Region

Roger C. Conner and Tony G. Johnson

Introduction

Cyclic price fluctuations in fossil fuels often result in renewed interest in developing and utilizing alternative sources of fuel to generate energy. Woody biomass as feedstock for biofuel is one source that has been considered in the past.

Logging residue and the biomass in standing residual inventory trees—primarily rough and rotten trees left on harvested sites—offer largely untapped potential as sources for a sustainable supply of biofuel. Rough trees are live trees of commercial species not containing at least one 12-foot saw log, or two noncontiguous saw logs, each 8 feet or longer, now or prospectively, primarily because of roughness, poor form, splits, cracks, and with less than one-third of the gross board-foot tree volume in sound material; and live trees of noncommercial species. Rotten trees are defined similarly, but have less than one-third of gross board-foot tree volume in sound material. This report provides estimates of post-harvest biomass in logging residue and residual inventory from timberland acres where tree cutting has occurred.

Biomass as Defined by FIA

Biomass as defined and reported by the U.S. Department of Agriculture Forest Service, Forest Inventory and Analysis (FIA) is the aboveground dry weight (in tons) of wood in the bole and limbs of live trees ≥ 1-inch diameter at breast height (d.b.h.). The bole is that portion of a tree between a 1-foot stump and a 4-inch top diameter outside bark (d.o.b.). FIA's biomass estimates, derived from equations developed by Clark and Saucier (1990) and Saucier and Clark (1985), exclude tree foliage, seedlings, and understory vegetation (U.S. Department of Agriculture Forest Service 2004).

For live residual trees, the dry weight estimates of biomass were doubled to convert to green weight. For harvested trees, cubic-foot removal volumes (including logging residue) were converted to green tons using 69.54 pounds per cubic foot for softwoods and 75.33 pounds per cubic foot for hardwoods. These conversions were derived from the relationship between the biomass in the merchantable portion of the tree (1-foot stump to a 4-inch d.o.b. top) and the cubic-foot volume in that portion. Green weight is the wood and bark per cubic foot of volume immediately after felling, when the tree's moisture content is high. Severed trees lose moisture rapidly, resulting in a significant drop in weight in a short amount of time.

Logging Residue

Logging residue is a component of FIA's estimates of total timber removals. FIA defines timber removals as the cubic-foot volume in trees ≥ 5.0 inches d.b.h. harvested for products; whole trees or portions of trees (tops, limbs, and bark) left behind as logging residue; and trees removed due to land clearing or other changes in land use. Also included is the biomass in trees 1.0-4.9 inches d.b.h. killed during logging operations. Estimates of average total removals, annual roundwood product output, logging residue, and other removals are reported in green tons for the most recent inventory of each Southern State.

FIA calculates the merchantable portion (bole) of logging residue as the volume from a 1-foot stump to a 4-inch top (d.o.b.) of whole trees cut and not utilized. Underutilization factors derived from felled-tree utilization studies are applied to this volume for the remainder of the merchantable portion of logging residue (Bentley and Johnson 2008). Factors derived from standing inventory data and utilization studies are applied to the merchantable portion of logging residue to calculate the nongrowing-stock portion in tops, limbs, and stumps.

Studies suggest a 60-percent recovery rate of logging residue is a realistic goal for harvesting operations using conventional equipment (Perlack and others 2005). Estimates of available logging residue presented in this report reflect this plausible rate of recovery.

Residual Inventory

Biomass in residual inventory is the volume (in weight) of standing live trees left after tree cutting activity. On final harvest acres, estimates of biomass include all-live standing residual trees (≥ 1.0-inch d.b.h.) left after harvest. On all other acres with evidence of tree cutting, estimates of biomass include only rough and rotten trees (≥ 1.0-inch d.b.h.) remaining in the standing inventory after the cutting activity.

Types of Cutting

Estimates of biomass in logging residue and standing residuals are from timberland acres that have undergone some form of stand treatment, i.e. there is evidence of tree cutting. Types of cutting range from final harvests where > 50 percent of the stand stocking is removed, to timber stand improvement where small-diameter trees are removed from immature stands to improve future stocking. FIA identifies five types of cutting:

final harvest: removal of the majority of merchantable trees, residual stocking is < 50 percent;

partial harvest: removal primarily consisting of higher quality trees due to high grading or selection harvest;

seed-tree/shelterwood: crop trees harvested leaving seed source trees for future stand;

commercial thinning: typically removal of poletimber-size trees from poletimber stands leaving sufficient stocking of growing-stock trees to feature in future stand development; and

timber stand improvement: cleaning, release, or other stand improvement involving noncommercial cutting applied to an immature stand that leaves sufficient stocking.

Survey Years

The biomass estimates in this report are based on data from recent surveys conducted in the 13 Southern States. Data collection occurred over a range of years for each State:

State	Survey year	Measurement year
Alabama	2008	2001–08
Arkansas	2005	1996–2005
Florida	2007	2002–07
Georgia	2008	1998–2008
Kentucky	2007	1999–2007
Louisiana	2005	2001–05
Mississippi	2006	1995–2006
North Carolina	2007	2002–07
Oklahoma	2008	1994–2008
South Carolina	2007	2001–07
Tennessee	2007	1999–2007
Texas	2008	2003–08
Virginia	2007	2002–07

The tree cutting and the resulting estimates of logging residue and residual biomass from harvested acres occurred over a 14-year period (1994–2008). The number of acres and types of cutting vary from State to State and from year to year. This variability complicates estimates of biomass availability. However, the estimates of logging residue and residual inventory for each State do provide a general estimate of what levels might be expected given typical harvest activity in the region.

Logging a hardwood site in Arkansas. (photo by Tony G. Johnson)

2

Logging a hardwood site in North Georgia. (photo by Tony G. Johnson)

Results

Estimates of timberland acres by type of cutting, biomass in logging residue, and residual inventory are summarized and briefly discussed at the regional level. Detailed estimates for individual States and ownerships are provided in the appendix tables.

Total timberland area with evidence of tree cutting averaged just over 6.0 million acres annually for all 13 Southern States over the 14-year period from 1994 to 2008 (table 1). Final harvest was the primary type of cutting and averaged almost 2.3 million acres annually. Partial harvest and commercial thinning accounted for 1.7 million acres, and 1.8 million acres, respectively. Combined, seed-tree/shelterwood cutting and timber stand improvement cutting averaged to 215,000 acres. Estimates of biomass in logging residue and residual inventory are a result of tree cutting on these acres.

Table 1—Annual timberland acres with tree cutting and the biomass in standing residual trees after harvest, the South, 1994–2008

Type of cutting	Annual timberland acres	Biomass in residual inventory trees
	thousand	*thousand green tons*
Final harvest	2,298.5	456,956
Partial harvest	1,704.2	75,007
Commercial thinning	1,798.3	193,423
Seed-tree/shelterwood	100.9	4,489
Timber stand improvement	114.1	7,151
Total	6,016.0	737,026

As a result of annual tree cutting of all types in all 13 Southern States, a total of > 737 million green tons of residual biomass in standing live trees remained after harvesting (table 1). Of that volume, biomass in all-live residual inventory trees (≥ 1.0-inch d.b.h.) on all final harvest acres amounted to nearly 457 million green tons. Biomass in rough and rotten trees from all other cutting combined totaled just over 280 million green tons.

Table 2 shows the distribution of recoverable logging residue for softwood and hardwood biomass combined. Recall the accepted recovery rate was set at 60 percent of the biomass in logging residue produced during harvest operations. The estimates in table 2 do not include stump volume which is considered unrecoverable. Based on expert opinion, the logging residue from nonmerchantable trees (< 5.0 inches d.b.h.) killed during the logging was adjusted to include only 20 percent as recoverable biomass (Lupold 2008).

With those adjustments, loggers could potentially recover almost 62.9 million green tons of biomass generated from all types of cutting activity in all 13 States. The bulk of the recoverable biomass (55.1 million green tons) would come from the harvest of trees > 5.0 inches d.b.h.

Table 2—Green weight of recoverable logging residue by size class of harvested trees, the South, 1995–2008

Size class of harvested trees	Recoverable logging residue in harvested trees[a]		
	Merchantable[b]	Non-merchantable[c]	Total
inches	*thousand green tons*		
> 5	25,868	29,194	55,062
< 5	0	7,830	7,830
All trees	25,868	37,023	62,891

Numbers in rows and columns may not sum to totals due to rounding.

[a] Green weight of logging residue assumes a maximum of 60 percent of total residue produced is recoverable.

[b] For harvested trees ≥ 5.0 inches diameter at breast height (d.b.h.), the volume in the bole from a 1-foot stump to a 4-inch top.

[c] For harvested trees ≥ 5.0 inches d.b h., it is the volume in the portion of the tree above a 4-inch top, and the volume in limbs to a 1-inch end diameter. Also includes total volume (from 1-foot stump to a 1-inch top diameter) of trees < 5.0 inches d.b.h.

Summary

Tree cutting activities can leave a wide ranging amount of biomass in logging residue and standing residuals. Harvest activity of all types in all 13 Southern States occurring between 1994 and 2008 resulted in an estimated 799.9 million green tons of biomass in logging residue and residual inventory, combined (tables A.1 and A.2). This unutilized material could be harvested as part of the original logging operation, eliminating the need for a costly second site visit. In addition, harvesting logging residue and standing residuals would leave a much cleaner site, reducing site prep and planting costs.

If recovered, this material could be used to help supply a biofuels industry in the South. However, collecting and transporting biomass are difficult and costly processes for loggers to undertake. Moreover, specialized equipment such as chippers, grinders, and chip vans would likely be needed to recover the material.

Logging residue is currently not utilized for a variety of reasons, including the general lack of markets. The recent upswing in fossil fuel prices could renew interest in biofuels and help create those markets (Scott and Tiarks 2008, Straka and others 2004). Increased demand would result in higher prices per delivered ton, making harvesting biomass a financially viable activity for loggers and create an additional source of income for forest landowners.

Literature Cited

Bentley, J.W.; Johnson, T.G. 2008. South Carolina harvest and utilization study, 2006. Resour. Bull. SRS–140. Asheville, NC: U.S. Department of Agriculture Forest Service, Southern Research Station. 24 p.

Clark, A., III; Saucier, J.R. 1990. Tables for estimating total tree weights, stem weights, and volumes of planted and natural southern pines in the Southeast. Georgia For. Res. Pap. 79. Georgia Forestry Commission, Research Division. 23 p.

Lupold, H.M. (Mac). 2008. [Personal communication]. Oct. 3. Columbia, SC: Lupold Consulting, Inc.

Perlack, R.D.; Wright, L.L.; Turhollow, A. [and others]. 2005. Biomass as feedstock for a bioenergy and bioproducts industry: the technical feasibility of a billion-ton annual supply. ORNL/TM–2005/66. Washington, DC: U.S. Department of Energy and U.S. Department of Agriculture Forest Service. 73 p.

Saucier, J.R.; Clark, A., III. 1985. Tables for estimating total tree and product weight and volume of major southern tree species and species groups. Washington, DC: Southwide Energy Committee, American Pulpwood Association. 59 p.

Scott, D.A.; Tiarks, A. 2008. Dual-cropping loblolly pine for biomass energy and conventional wood products. Southern Journal of Applied Forestry. 32(1): 33–37.

Straka, T.J.; Irwin, H.T.; Adams, T.O. 2004. Small-diameter timber: problem or opportunity? Carolina Forestry Journal. July: 4–5.

U.S. Department of Agriculture Forest Service. 2004. Forest inventory and analysis national core field guide: field data collection procedures for phase 2 plots. Version 2.0. Washington, DC. 208 p. Vol. I. Internal report. On file with: U.S. Department of Agriculture Forest Service, Forest Inventory and Analysis, 201 14th Street, Washington, DC 20250.

Appendix

Index of Tables

Table A.1—Annual timberland acres with tree cutting, by ownership class and type of cutting, the South, 1994–2008

Table A.2—Annual timberland acres with tree cutting, by State and type of cutting, 1994–2008

Table A.3—Annual timberland acres with tree cutting, by State, ownership class, and type of cutting, 1994–2008

Table A.4—Green weight of biomass in standing residual inventory trees on timberland acres with tree cutting, by ownership class and type of cutting, the South, 1994–2008

Table A.5—Green weight of biomass in standing residual inventory trees on timberland acres with tree cutting, by State and type of cutting, 1994–2008

Table A.6—Green weight of biomass in residual inventory trees on timberland acres with tree cutting, by State, ownership class, and type of cutting, 1994–2008

Table A.7—Green weight of biomass in residual inventory trees on timberland acres with tree cutting, by State, species group, and diameter class, 1994–2008

Table A.8—Annual timberland acres with tree cutting and the biomass in residual inventory trees after cutting, by State and type of cutting, 1994–2008

Table A.9—Green weight of recoverable logging residue by State, 1995–2008

Table A.10—Green weight of softwood recoverable logging residue by State, 1995–2008

Table A.11—Green weight of hardwood recoverable logging residue by State, 1995–2008

Table A.12—Volume of timber removals by removals class, species group, and source, the South, 1995–2008

Table A.13—Green weight of timber removals by removals class, species group, and source, the South, 1995–2008

Table A.14—Green weight of timber removals by removals class, species group, and source, Alabama, 2001–08

Table A.15—Green weight of timber removals by removals class, species group, and source, Arkansas, 1996–2004

Table A.16—Green weight of timber removals by removals class, species group, and source, Florida, 1995–2007

Table A.17—Green weight of timber removals by removals class, species group, and source, Georgia, 1997–2008

Table A.18—Green weight of timber removals by removals class, species group, and source, Kentucky, 1988–2007

Table A.19—Green weight of timber removals by removals class, species group, and source, Louisiana, 1991–2003

Table A.20—Green weight of timber removals by removals class, species group, and source, Mississippi, 1995–2005

Table A.21—Green weight of timber removals by removals class, species group, and source, North Carolina, 2002–07

Table A.22—Green weight of timber removals by removals class, species group, and source, Oklahoma (east), 1994–2008

Table A.23—Green weight of timber removals by removals class, species group, and source, South Carolina, 2001–07

Table A.24—Green weight of timber removals by removals class, species group, and source, Tennessee, 1999–2007

Table A.25—Green weight of timber removals by removals class, species group, and source, Texas (east), 2003–07

Table A.26—Green weight of timber removals by removals class, species group, and source, Virginia, 2002–07

Table A.1 — Annual timberland acres with tree cutting, by ownership class and type of cutting, the South, 1994–2008

Ownership class	Type of cutting					All cutting
	Final harvest	Commercial thinning	Partial harvest	Seed-tree/ shelterwood	Timber stand improvement	
	thousand acres					
National forest	13.7	30.3	34.5	7.4	15.4	101.2
Other public	52.0	41.3	50.1	1.8	10.0	155.2
Forest industry	616.2	461.1	230.7	19.3	17.9	1,345.2
Private	1,616.7	1,171.5	1,483.0	72.5	70.8	4,414.5
Total	2,298.5	1,704.2	1,798.2	100.9	114.1	6,015.9

Numbers in rows and columns may not sum to totals due to rounding.

Table A.2 — Annual timberland acres with tree cutting, by State and type of cutting, 1994–2008

State	Type of cutting					All cutting
	Final harvest	Commercial thinning	Partial harvest	Seed-tree/ shelterwood	Timber stand improvement	
	thousand acres					
Alabama	366.4	275.2	164.6	14.9	15.6	836.7
Arkansas	164.2	138.5	263.2	8.5	25.9	600.2
Florida	190.6	61.9	69.1	3.3	5.5	330.5
Georgia	296.1	316.6	129.3	16.2	18.0	776.2
Kentucky	16.6	10.7	255.3	5.5	4.1	292.2
Louisiana	218.8	150.7	148.2	12.6	5.2	535.6
Mississippi	266.1	150.1	158.4	5.4	2.8	582.8
North Carolina	227.5	101.8	87.1	2.1	10.6	429.2
Oklahoma (east)	38.0	19.8	43.0	0.8	0.0	101.5
South Carolina	149.8	200.0	63.9	13.2	13.0	439.8
Tennessee	56.6	4.4	161.5	3.9	1.2	227.6
Texas (east)	174.4	219.4	136.8	11.9	1.9	544.3
Virginia	133.6	55.1	117.9	2.6	10.4	319.6
Total	2,298.5	1,704.2	1,798.3	100.9	114.1	6,016.0

Numbers in rows and columns may not sum to totals due to rounding.

0.0 = no sample for the cell or a value > 0.0 but < 0.05.

Table A.3—Annual timberland acres with tree cutting, by State, ownership class, and type of cutting, 1994–2008

State and ownership class	Type of cutting					
	Final harvest	Commercial thinning	Partial harvest	Seed-tree/ shelterwood	Timber stand improvement	All cutting
	thousand acres					
Alabama						
National forest	1.0	0.0	0.0	0.0	0.7	1.6
Other public	5.1	3.5	2.5	0.0	0.0	11.1
Forest industry	87.0	58.3	14.3	5.8	1.0	166.4
Private	273.3	213.4	147.8	9.1	14.0	657.6
Total	366.4	275.2	164.6	14.9	15.6	836.7
Arkansas						
National forest	1.3	12.1	13.4	3.0	10.3	40.1
Other public	0.2	3.4	4.6	0.0	1.7	10.0
Forest industry	97.0	66.1	72.0	3.1	5.8	243.9
Private	65.7	56.9	173.2	2.4	8.1	306.3
Total	164.2	138.5	263.2	8.5	25.9	600.2
Florida						
National forest	3.8	0.5	0.9	0.7	0.0	5.9
Other public	20.4	8.5	7.3	0.7	1.6	38.4
Forest industry	35.6	4.0	4.3	0.0	0.9	44.8
Private	130.8	49.0	56.7	1.9	3.1	241.4
Total	190.6	61.9	69.1	3.3	5.5	330.5
Georgia						
National forest	0.4	0.4	0.0	1.3	0.6	2.7
Other public	6.3	7.1	5.8	0.0	1.7	20.8
Forest industry	79.5	49.5	10.0	2.4	5.0	146.3
Private	210.0	259.6	113.6	12.5	10.8	606.4
Total	296.1	316.6	129.3	16.2	18.0	776.2
Kentucky						
National forest	0.0	0.0	2.3	0.0	0.0	2.3
Other public	0.4	1.2	4.3	0.0	0.9	6.9
Forest industry	0.9	1.4	5.6	0.0	0.7	8.5
Private	15.3	8.1	243.0	5.5	2.5	274.5
Total	16.6	10.7	255.3	5.5	4.1	292.2
Louisiana						
National forest	1.4	6.1	5.6	0.0	1.3	14.4
Other public	1.5	0.2	8.2	0.0	0.0	10.0
Forest industry	106.5	88.4	41.0	4.8	3.42	244.1
Private	109.5	56.0	93.3	7.8	0.43	267.1
Total	218.8	150.7	148.2	12.6	5.2	535.5
Mississippi						
National forest	3.2	3.6	8.6	0.9	0.0	16.2
Other public	6.1	2.3	5.8	0.0	0.5	14.6
Forest industry	44.3	31.9	15.1	0.4	0.0	91.7
Private	212.5	112.4	128.9	4.1	2.4	460.2
Total	266.1	150.1	158.4	5.4	2.8	582.8

continued

Table A.3—Annual timberland acres with tree cutting, by State, ownership class, and type of cutting, 1994–2008 (continued)

State and ownership class	Type of cutting					All cutting
	Final harvest	Commercial thinning	Partial harvest	Seed-tree/ shelterwood	Timber stand improvement	
	thousand acres					
North Carolina						
National forest	0.0	0.0	0.0	1.6	2.6	4.1
Other public	2.4	6.6	0.7	0.0	0.0	9.7
Forest industry	34.8	35.1	12.9	0.0	1.2	84.1
Private	190.3	60.1	73.5	0.5	6.8	331.3
Total	227.5	101.8	87.1	2.1	10.6	429.2
Oklahoma (east)						
National forest	0.0	1.5	1.1	0.0	0.0	2.6
Other public	0.0	0.0	0.8	0.0	0.0	0.8
Forest industry	16.2	8.5	2.1	0.0	0.0	26.8
Private	21.8	9.8	39.0	0.8	0.0	71.3
Total	38.0	19.8	43.0	0.8	0.0	101.5
South Carolina						
National forest	0.1	3.7	0.2	0.0	0.0	4.0
Other public	4.8	5.9	1.7	1.1	3.7	17.2
Forest industry	27.5	22.7	9.4	0.0	0.0	59.6
Private	117.4	167.7	52.6	12.1	9.3	359.0
Total	149.8	200.0	63.9	13.2	13.0	439.8
Tennessee						
National forest	0.0	0.0	1.0	0.0	0.0	1.0
Other public	1.7	0.0	5.2	0.0	0.0	7.0
Forest industry	13.6	1.4	10.5	0.0	0.0	25.5
Private	41.3	3.0	144.7	3.9	1.2	194.1
Total	56.6	4.4	161.5	3.9	1.2	227.5
Texas (east)						
National forest	0.0	2.3	0.0	0.0	0.0	2.3
Other public	0.2	0.0	0.4	0.0	0.0	0.6
Forest industry	60.1	87.8	19.6	2.7	0.0	170.2
Private	114.1	129.3	116.7	9.2	1.9	371.2
Total	174.4	219.4	136.8	11.9	1.9	544.3
Virginia						
National forest	2.6	0.0	1.3	0.0	0.0	3.9
Other public	2.9	2.6	2.7	0.0	0.0	8.1
Forest industry	13.3	6.1	13.9	0.0	0.0	33.3
Private	114.8	46.4	100.0	2.6	10.4	274.2
Total	133.6	55.1	117.9	2.6	10.4	319.6
All States						
National forest	13.7	30.3	34.5	7.4	15.4	101.2
Other public	52.0	41.3	50.1	1.8	10.0	155.2
Forest industry	616.2	461.1	230.7	19.3	17.9	1,345.2
Private	1,616.7	1,171.5	1,483.0	72.5	70.8	4,414.5
Total	2,298.5	1,704.2	1,798.2	100.9	114.1	6,015.9

Numbers in rows and columns may not sum to totals due to rounding.

0.0 = no sample for the cell or a value > 0.0 but < 0.05.

Table A.4—Green weight of biomass in standing residual inventory trees on timberland acres with tree cutting, by ownership class and type of cutting, the South, 1994–2008

| Ownership class | Type of cutting | | | | | |
	Final harvest[a]	Commercial thinning	Partial harvest	Seed-tree/ shelterwood	Timber stand improvement	All cutting
	green tons					
National forest	3,058,432	1,497,049	2,933,543	221,667	884,975	8,595,666
Other public	8,034,426	1,512,763	5,872,901	6,213	622,001	16,048,305
Forest industry	96,805,832	15,953,401	15,871,654	455,276	203,293	129,289,457
Private	349,057,003	56,043,949	168,744,777	3,805,579	5,440,852	583,092,161
Total	456,955,694	75,007,163	193,422,875	4,488,735	7,151,122	737,025,588

Numbers in rows and columns may not sum to totals due to rounding.

[a] For final harvest acres standing residual inventory includes the biomass in live trees ≥ 1.0-inch d.b h. For all other cutting standing residual inventory includes only rough and rotten trees ≥ 1.0-inch d b.h.

Table A.5—Green weight of biomass in standing residual inventory trees on timberland acres with tree cutting, by State and type of cutting, 1994–2008

| State | Type of cutting | | | | | |
	Final harvest[a]	Commercial thinning	Partial harvest	Seed-tree/ shelterwood	Timber stand improvement	All cutting
	green tons					
Alabama	92,635,050	13,440,342	15,295,299	527,190	827,880	122,725,761
Arkansas	11,432,001	4,677,250	19,137,790	272,051	1,060,81	36,579,905
Florida	19,140,348	1,691,902	9,824,545	31,524	590,953	31,279,272
Georgia	137,130,761	13,460,480	13,737,496	863,572	728,414	165,920,722
Kentucky	4,757,110	1,120,672	34,381,706	400,730	502,403	41,162,622
Louisiana	35,470,815	5,946,774	17,042,359	993,875	90,093	59,543,915
Mississippi	83,682,236	13,492,240	29,291,962	299,022	983,772	127,749,232
North Carolina	11,017,841	2,432,158	4,285,963	23,576	412,072	18,171,610
Oklahoma (east)	7,347,535	3,038,150	10,667,759	192,046	0	21,245,490
South Carolina	21,501,230	8,907,719	3,682,025	530,618	311,180	34,932,772
Tennessee	21,955,229	812,545	21,675,923	113,389	843,622	45,400,707
Texas (east)	4,082,436	4,343,807	3,836,019	66,495	18,110	12,346,866
Virginia	6,803,103	1,643,124	10,564,029	174,645	781,809	19,966,710
Total	456,955,694	75,007,163	193,422,875	4,488,733	7,151,120	737,025,584

Numbers in rows and columns may not sum to totals due to rounding.

[a] For final harvest acres standing residual inventory includes the biomass in live trees ≥ 1.0-inch d.b h. For all other cutting standing residual inventory includes only rough and rotten trees ≥ 1.0-inch d.b.h.

Table A.6—Green weight of biomass in residual inventory trees on timberland acres with tree cutting, by State, ownership class, and type of cutting, 1994–2008

State and ownership class	Type of cutting					
	Final harvest[a]	Commercial thinning	Partial harvest	Seed-tree/ shelterwood	Timber stand improvement	All cutting
	green tons					
Alabama						
National forest	281,605	0	0	0	21,627	303,233
Other public	1,119,220	532,253	688,538	0	0	2,340,011
Forest industry	19,387,989	2,607,059	941,862	165,757	15,974	23,118,641
Private	71,846,235	10,301,031	13,664,900	361,432	790,278	96,963,877
Total	92,635,050	13,440,342	15,295,299	527,190	827,880	122,725,761
Arkansas						
National forest	183,630	243,603	326,433	129,375	565,385	1,448,426
Other public	0	112,214	604,683	0	51,556	768,453
Forest industry	4,385,682	1,966,725	4,735,715	61,122	85,184	11,234,429
Private	6,862,689	2,354,707	13,470,960	81,554	358,687	23,128,597
Total	11,432,001	4,677,250	19,137,790	272,051	1,060,813	36,579,905
Florida						
National forest	267,120	25,989	20,304	0	0	313,413
Other public	1,725,839	252,797	633,712	6,213	221,171	2,839,731
Forest industry	2,975,609	32,010	554,021	0	0	3,561,640
Private	14,171,780	1,381,106	8,616,508	25,313	369,784	24,564,491
Total	19,140,348	1,691,902	9,824,545	31,526	590,955	31,279,276
Georgia						
National forest	420,975	25,342	0	6,091	16,620	469,027
Other public	2,127,292	112,606	203,390	0	766	2,444,054
Forest industry	33,921,211	1,822,214	1,347,762	122,470	13,925	37,227,582
Private	100,661,284	11,500,318	12,186,345	735,011	697,103	125,780,059
Total	137,130,761	13,460,480	13,737,496	863,572	728,414	165,920,722
Kentucky						
National forest	0	0	455,317	0	0	455,317
Other public	23,795	38,732	944,348	0	96,253	1,103,128
Forest industry	0	5,475	246,834	0	0	252,309
Private	4,733,316	1,076,465	32,735,206	400,730	406,151	39,351,868
Total	4,757,110	1,120,672	34,381,706	400,730	502,403	41,162,622
Louisiana						
National forest	426,962	196,311	384,224	0	1,883	1,009,380
Other public	147,654	0	1,091,743	0	0	1,239,398
Forest industry	13,427,697	2,946,452	3,570,817	81,048	88,209	20,114,223
Private	21,468,502	2,804,011	11,995,575	912,827	0	37,180,915
Total	35,470,815	5,946,774	17,042,359	993,875	90,093	59,543,915
Mississippi						
National forest	1,271,743	589,725	1,026,269	64,681	0	2,952,418
Other public	1,436,485	110,266	881,142	0	222,467	2,650,360
Forest industry	10,612,481	3,059,823	1,468,428	24,017	0	15,164,748
Private	70,361,527	9,732,426	25,916,123	210,325	761,305	106,981,705
Total	83,682,236	13,492,240	29,291,962	299,022	983,772	127,749,232

continued

Table A.6—Green weight of biomass in residual inventory trees on timberland acres with tree cutting, by State, ownership class, and type of cutting, 1994–2008 (continued)

State and ownership class	Type of cutting					
	Final harvest[a]	Commercial thinning	Partial harvest	Seed-tree/ shelterwood	Timber stand improvement	All cutting
	green tons					
North Carolina						
National forest	0	0	0	21,521	279,459	300,980
Other public	2,100	169,981	0	0	0	172,081
Forest industry	2,356,520	588,866	781,470	0	0	3,726,855
Private	8,659,222	1,673,311	3,504,493	2,055	132,613	13,971,695
Total	11,017,841	2,432,158	4,285,963	23,576	412,072	18,171,610
Oklahoma (east)						
National forest	0	364,187	193,217	0	0	557,404
Other public	0	0	150,403	0	0	150,403
Forest industry	2,556,493	902,230	437,990	0	0	3,896,712
Private	4,791,042	1,771,733	9,886,149	192,046	0	16,640,971
Total	7,347,535	3,038,150	10,667,759	192,046	0	21,245,490
South Carolina						
National forest	0	40,466	0	0	0	40,466
Other public	260,343	146,747	16,967	0	29,788	453,846
Forest industry	2,656,212	490,905	197,422	0	0	3,344,539
Private	18,584,675	8,229,601	3,467,636	530,618	281,391	31,093,921
Total	21,501,230	8,907,719	3,682,025	530,618	311,180	34,932,772
Tennessee						
National forest	0	0	10,816	0	0	10,816
Other public	1,114,929	0	437,442	0	0	1,552,371
Forest industry	3,469,183	311,140	680,350	0	0	4,460,673
Private	17,371,116	501,406	20,547,315	113,389	843,622	39,376,847
Total	21,955,229	812,545	21,675,923	113,389	843,622	45,400,707
Texas (east)						
National forest	0	11,426	0	0	0	11,426
Other public	0	0	93,412	0	0	93,412
Forest industry	798,956	1,001,696	336,075	862	0	2,137,589
Private	3,283,479	3,330,685	3,406,532	65,633	18,110	10,104,439
Total	4,082,436	4,343,807	3,836,019	66,495	18,110	12,346,866
Virginia						
National forest	206,398	0	516,963	0	0	723,361
Other public	76,769	37,168	127,120	0	0	241,057
Forest industry	257,799	218,807	572,910	0	0	1,049,517
Private	6,262,136	1,387,149	9,347,037	174,645	781,809	17,952,775
Total	6,803,103	1,643,124	10,564,029	174,645	781,809	19,966,710
All States						
National forest	3,058,432	1,497,049	2,933,543	221,667	884,975	8,595,666
Other public	8,034,426	1,512,763	5,872,901	6,213	622,001	16,048,305
Forest industry	96,805,832	15,953,401	15,871,654	455,276	203,293	129,289,457
Private	349,057,003	56,043,949	168,744,777	3,805,579	5,440,852	583,092,161
Total	456,955,694	75,007,163	193,422,875	4,488,735	7,151,122	737,025,588

Numbers in rows and columns may not sum to totals due to rounding.

[a] For final harvest acres standing residual inventory includes the biomass in live trees ≥ 1 0-inch d.b.h. For all other cutting standing residual inventory includes only rough and rotten trees ≥ 1.0-inch d.b.h.

Table A.7—Green weight of biomass in residual inventory trees on timberland acres with tree cutting, by State, species group, and diameter class, 1994–2008

State and species group	All classes	Diameter class (inches)											
		1.0–2.9	3.0–4.9	5.0–6.9	7.0–8.9	9.0–10.9	11.0–12.9	13.0–14.9	15.0–16.9	17.0–18.9	19.0–20.9	21.0–28.9	≥29.0
		green tons[a]											
Alabama													
Softwood	52,957,146	1,140,590	2,275,841	4,811,003	7,882,574	9,160,529	7,628,959	6,286,933	5,829,450	3,144,745	1,404,896	3,391,627	0
Hardwood	69,768,615	9,978,496	8,383,937	7,207,294	7,464,699	6,817,163	7,108,801	6,105,026	4,720,787	3,832,228	3,020,486	3,323,751	1,805,945
All species	122,725,761	11,119,086	10,659,777	12,018,297	15,347,273	15,977,692	14,737,759	12,391,959	10,550,237	6,976,973	4,425,383	6,715,379	1,805,945
Arkansas													
Softwood	56,800,128	4,874,865	4,861,783	4,934,867	4,931,785	4,821,313	4,936,737	4,858,897	4,623,711	4,577,689	4,577,689	4,577,689	4,577,689
Hardwood	29,779,776	5,687,804	4,184,018	3,050,715	2,754,415	2,272,080	1,735,607	1,380,817	1,754,881	1,644,128	713,526	3,001,531	1,600,255
All species	86,579,905	10,562,670	9,045,801	7,985,582	7,686,200	7,093,393	6,672,344	6,239,714	6,378,592	6,221,817	5,291,215	7,579,220	6,177,944
Florida													
Softwood	14,731,132	2,035,903	5,875,979	3,854,126	1,540,269	540,689	278,125	144,648	150,560	128,367	0	182,469	0
Hardwood	16,548,143	2,002,912	1,701,920	1,508,025	1,415,618	811,552	1,174,371	800,167	789,836	360,545	708,539	1,619,059	3,655,600
All species	31,279,276	4,038,815	7,577,899	5,362,151	2,955,887	1,352,240	1,452,495	944,815	940,396	488,911	708,539	1,801,528	3,655,600
Georgia													
Softwood	88,522,765	1,375,476	3,578,246	11,364,818	18,234,650	17,492,134	12,882,478	7,412,823	6,038,174	3,865,834	1,051,506	4,558,618	668,011
Hardwood	77,397,957	8,887,058	9,824,642	7,301,106	6,920,495	7,615,048	6,878,576	7,226,988	5,588,819	3,425,118	3,809,793	5,439,529	4,480,783
All species	165,920,722	10,262,535	13,402,888	18,665,923	25,155,145	25,107,182	19,761,054	14,639,811	11,626,993	7,290,952	4,861,299	9,998,147	5,148,795
Kentucky													
Total softwood	2,835,736	100,876	336,490	454,672	428,101	300,998	149,588	118,129	383,515	190,862	372,507	0	0
Total hardwood	38,326,886	3,690,070	4,177,260	2,910,684	2,899,071	3,368,971	3,562,063	2,706,457	2,515,097	2,849,543	1,461,947	5,103,408	3,082,313
All species	41,162,622	3,790,946	4,513,750	3,365,356	3,327,172	3,669,970	3,711,652	2,824,585	2,898,612	3,040,405	1,834,454	5,103,408	3,082,313
Louisiana													
Softwood	20,346,387	2,272,871	5,599,779	5,363,962	2,375,300	1,107,479	616,754	858,597	623,581	286,018	602,286	639,765	0
Hardwood	39,197,528	7,337,079	5,259,835	3,279,149	2,830,299	2,487,190	1,936,504	2,255,862	2,165,801	1,999,433	1,767,593	4,782,171	3,096,613
All species	59,543,915	9,609,950	10,859,613	8,643,110	5,205,599	3,594,669	2,553,258	3,114,459	2,789,382	2,285,451	2,369,880	5,421,935	3,096,613
Mississippi													
Softwood	53,794,215	4,289,044	10,818,582	18,129,393	10,965,493	3,544,581	2,442,395	871,868	1,320,732	624,054	482,839	305,235	0
Hardwood	73,955,017	16,274,975	12,275,402	7,957,661	6,707,095	5,342,665	4,611,298	3,013,788	3,240,539	2,113,352	1,938,267	5,508,544	4,163,467
All species	127,749,232	20,564,019	23,093,984	26,087,054	17,672,588	8,887,245	7,053,693	3,885,655	4,561,271	2,737,406	2,421,106	5,813,779	4,163,467

continued

Table A.7—Green weight of biomass in residual inventory trees on timberland acres with tree cutting, by State, species group, and diameter class, 1994–2008 (continued)

State and species group	Diameter class (inches)												
	All classes	1.0–2.9	3.0–4.9	5.0–6.9	7.0–8.9	9.0–10.9	11.0–12.9	13.0–14.9	15.0–16.9	17.0–18.9	19.0–20.9	21.0–28.9	≥29.0
	green tons[a]												
North Carolina													
Softwood	3,551,858	471,706	346,093	326,569	426,156	543,618	529,960	510,808	39,895	70,215	0	286,840	0
Hardwood	14,619,752	2,652,313	2,202,842	1,646,598	1,528,970	1,344,611	1,039,531	981,655	797,445	483,569	560,968	485,332	895,918
All species	18,171,610	3,124,019	2,548,935	1,973,167	1,955,126	1,888,230	1,569,491	1,492,463	837,340	553,785	560,968	772,172	895,918
Oklahoma (east)													
Softwood	5,980,509	367,972	886,594	1,677,119	1,700,246	428,868	263,766	239,769	121,695	191,589	0	102,896	0
Hardwood	15,264,981	2,197,812	2,723,300	1,923,439	1,835,786	1,725,941	1,166,787	1,307,354	891,991	484,089	344,957	330,414	333,112
All species	21,245,490	2,565,784	3,609,894	3,600,557	3,536,033	2,154,809	1,430,553	1,547,124	1,013,685	675,678	344,957	433,310	333,112
South Carolina													
Softwood	12,534,331	345,789	736,215	1,192,593	2,157,770	2,682,327	1,702,018	501,589	713,085	914,600	795,451	430,586	362,310
Hardwood	22,398,442	3,259,011	3,194,178	2,179,493	1,864,307	1,758,289	2,138,466	1,702,106	1,805,172	1,277,409	750,618	1,469,247	1,000,146
All species	34,932,772	3,604,800	3,930,392	3,372,086	4,022,077	4,440,615	3,840,484	2,203,695	2,518,257	2,192,009	1,546,069	1,899,833	1,362,456
Tennessee													
Softwood	8,345,439	179,511	441,546	1,026,346	1,935,674	1,505,654	959,713	1,225,785	559,689	272,250	239,271	0	0
Hardwood	37,055,268	3,197,049	4,788,916	3,456,378	4,007,257	3,146,470	3,577,663	4,301,669	3,165,841	1,726,842	787,455	3,319,960	1,579,766
All species	45,400,707	3,376,560	5,230,462	4,482,724	5,942,932	4,652,124	4,537,376	5,527,455	3,725,531	1,999,092	1,026,725	3,319,960	1,579,766
Texas (east)													
Softwood	1,529,978	129,018	140,025	264,365	180,544	297,747	212,967	150,137	0	68,543	86,637	0	0
Hardwood	10,816,888	2,413,132	1,839,149	1,098,573	939,582	630,773	457,560	490,940	480,534	215,024	227,426	1,583,332	440,865
All species	12,346,866	2,542,150	1,979,174	1,362,938	1,120,126	928,520	670,527	641,077	480,534	283,567	314,063	1,583,332	440,865
Virginia													
Softwood	1,817,235	213,826	271,018	215,998	311,934	357,863	165,790	146,102	51,507	83,202	0	0	0
Hardwood	18,149,476	2,138,407	1,900,190	2,019,883	2,178,900	2,187,136	1,888,978	1,313,026	1,173,135	586,921	632,006	990,633	1,140,261
All species	19,966,710	2,352,232	2,171,208	2,235,881	2,490,834	2,544,999	2,054,767	1,459,128	1,224,642	670,123	632,006	990,633	1,140,261
All States													
Softwood	273,746,860	17,797,447	36,168,189	53,615,829	53,070,497	42,783,798	32,769,251	23,326,085	20,455,594	14,417,969	9,613,083	14,475,726	5,608,011
Hardwood	463,278,728	69,716,119	62,455,587	45,538,997	43,346,494	39,507,888	37,276,204	33,585,855	29,089,879	20,998,202	16,723,581	36,956,912	27,275,044
All species	737,025,588	87,513,566	98,623,776	99,154,826	96,416,991	82,291,686	70,045,454	56,911,939	49,545,473	35,416,171	26,336,664	51,432,638	32,883,055

Numbers in rows and columns may not sum to totals due to rounding.

[a] For final harvest acres standing residual inventory includes the biomass in live trees ≥ 1.0-inch d.b.h. For all other cutting standing residual inventory includes only rough and rotten trees ≥ 1.0-inch d.b.h.

Table A.8—Annual timberland acres with tree cutting and the biomass in residual inventory trees after cutting, by State and type of cutting, 1994–2008

State and type of cutting	Annual acres	Biomass in residual inventory trees[a]		State and type of cutting	Annual acres	Biomass in residual inventory trees[a]	
	thousand	*green tons per acre*	*thousand green tons per year*		*thousand*	*green tons per acre*	*thousand green tons per year*
Alabama				Louisiana			
Final harvest	366.4	49	17,952	Final harvest	218.8	15	3,286
Partial harvest	164.6	18	2,966	Partial harvest	148.2	11	1,689
Seed-tree/shelterwood	14.9	8	112	Seed-tree/shelterwood	12.6	8	105
Commercial thinning	275.2	10	2,761	Commercial thinning	150.7	4	631
Timber stand improvement	15.6	10	155	Timber stand improvement	5.2	2	9
Total	836.7		23,946	Total	535.5		5,720
Arkansas				Mississippi			
Final harvest	164.2	9	1,506	Final harvest	266.1	25	6,666
Partial harvest	263.2	10	2,560	Partial harvest	158.4	15	2,445
Seed-tree/shelterwood	8.5	4	35	Seed-tree/shelterwood	5.4	5	27
Commercial thinning	138.5	5	651	Commercial thinning	150.1	8	1,185
Timber stand improvement	25.9	6	158	Timber stand improvement	2.8	26	74
Total	600.2		4,910	Total	582.8		10,396
Florida				North Carolina			
Final harvest	190.6	10	1,930	Final harvest	227.5	9	2,139
Partial harvest	69.1	14	998	Partial harvest	87.1	12	1,006
Seed-tree/shelterwood	3.3	1	3	Seed-tree/shelterwood	2.1	3	6
Commercial thinning	61.9	3	164	Commercial thinning	101.8	4	449
Timber stand improvement	5.5	11	60	Timber stand improvement	10.6	10	103
Total	330.5		3,155	Total	429.2		3,703
Georgia				Oklahoma (east)			
Final harvest	296.1	90	26,713	Final harvest	38.0	14	537
Partial harvest	129.3	20	2,626	Partial harvest	43.0	18	761
Seed-tree/shelterwood	16.2	11	180	Seed-tree/shelterwood	0.8	16	13
Commercial thinning	316.6	8	2,614	Commercial thinning	19.8	11	219
Timber stand improvement	18.0	11	194	Timber stand improvement	0.0	0	0
Total	776.2		32,328	Total	101.5		1,530
Kentucky				South Carolina			
Final harvest	16.6	61	1,013	Final harvest	149.8	30	4,492
Partial harvest	255.3	29	7,430	Partial harvest	63.9	13	803
Seed-tree/shelterwood	5.5	17	94	Seed-tree/shelterwood	13.2	9	113
Commercial thinning	10.7	23	251	Commercial thinning	200.0	9	1,883
Timber stand improvement	4.1	23	96	Timber stand improvement	13.0	5	68
Total	292.2		8,885	Total	439.8		7,359

continued

Table A.8—Annual timberland acres with tree cutting and the biomass in residual inventory trees after cutting, by State and type of cutting, 1994–2008 (continued)

State and type of cutting	Annual acres	Biomass in residual inventory trees[a]		State and type of cutting	Annual acres	Biomass in residual inventory trees[a]	
	thousand	*green tons per acre*	*thousand green tons per year*		*thousand*	*green tons per acre*	*thousand green tons per year*
Tennessee				Virginia			
Final harvest	56.6	70	3,986	Final harvest	133.6	10	1,380
Partial harvest	161.5	25	3,985	Partial harvest	117.9	20	2,304
Seed-tree/shelterwood	3.9	4	17	Seed-tree/shelterwood	2.6	12	31
Commercial thinning	4.4	33	144	Commercial thinning	55.1	6	357
Timber stand improvement	1.2	151	175	Timber stand improvement	10.4	22	232
Total	227.6		8,307	Total	319.6		4,304
Texas (east)				All States			
Final harvest	174.4	7	1,193	Final harvest	2,298.5	NA	72,794
Partial harvest	136.8	8	1,113	Partial harvest	1,798.3	NA	30,685
Seed-tree/shelterwood	11.9	2	21	Seed-tree/shelterwood	100.9	NA	756
Commercial thinning	219.4	6	1,291	Commercial thinning	1,704.2	NA	12,600
Timber stand improvement	1.9	2	4	Timber stand improvement	114.1	NA	1,328
Total	544.3		3,622	Total	6,016.0		118,164

NA = not applicable.

[a] For final harvest acres standing residual inventory includes the biomass in live trees ≥ 1.0-inch d.b.h. For all other cutting standing residual inventory includes only rough and rotten trees ≥ 1.0-inch d.b.h.

Table A.9—Green weight of recoverable logging residue by State, 1995–2008

State	Size class of harvested trees	Recoverable logging residue in harvested trees[a] Merchantable[b]	Non-merchantable[c]	Total	Tons per acre	Total tons per acre
	inches		*green tons*			
Alabama	> 5	2,234,732	4,183,694	6,418,426	7.671	14.102
	< 5	0	1,533,394	1,533,394	1.833	1.833
	All trees	2,234,732	5,717,088	7,951,820	9.504	15.935
Arkansas	> 5	2,425,034	2,839,876	5,264,910	8.771	15.018
	< 5	0	340,598	340,598	0.567	2.837
	All trees	2,425,034	3,180,474	5,605,508	9.339	17.855
Florida	> 5	1,282,277	948,498	2,230,775	6.750	12.595
	< 5	0	619,389	619,389	1.874	1.874
	All trees	1,282,277	1,567,887	2,850,164	8.624	14.469
Georgia	> 5	2,664,347	3,488,159	6,152,506	7.927	14.371
	< 5	0	1,359,689	1,359,689	1.752	8.759
	All trees	2,664,347	4,847,848	7,512,195	9.679	23.130
Kentucky	> 5	2,261,579	1,742,417	4,003,996	13.704	23.403
	< 5	0	235,979	235,979	0.808	0.808
	All trees	2,261,579	1,978,396	4,239,975	14.512	24.211
Louisiana	> 5	2,943,617	2,804,053	5,747,670	10.580	18.690
	< 5	0	819,126	819,126	1.508	1.508
	All trees	2,943,617	3,623,179	6,566,796	12.088	20.198
Mississippi	> 5	2,582,667	2,395,683	4,978,350	6.583	14.948
	< 5	0	538,664	538,664	0.929	0.929
	All trees	2,582,667	2,934,347	5,517,014	9.512	15.877
North Carolina	> 5	2,429,605	3,028,189	5,457,794	12.717	21.987
	< 5	0	479,159	479,159	1.117	1.117
	All trees	2,429,605	3,507,348	5,936,953	13.834	23.104
Oklahoma (east)	> 5	258,995	219,073	478,068	4.691	8.519
	< 5	0	102,624	102,624	1.007	1.007
	All trees	258,995	321,697	580,692	5.698	9.526
South Carolina	> 5	1,530,963	2,658,961	4,189,924	9.474	16.771
	< 5	0	583,485	583,485	1.319	1.319
	All trees	1,530,963	3,242,446	4,773,409	10.793	18.090
Tennessee	> 5	1,456,669	1,148,166	2,604,835	11.447	19.847
	< 5	0	300,510	300,510	1.321	1.321
	All trees	1,456,669	1,448,676	2,905,345	12.768	21.168
Texas (east)	> 5	1,475,700	1,629,523	3,105,223	5.692	10.078
	< 5	0	482,760	482,760	0.885	0.885
	All trees	1,475,700	2,112,283	3,587,983	6.577	10.963
Virginia	> 5	2,321,834	2,107,247	4,429,081	13.858	24.004
	< 5	0	434,141	434,141	1.358	1.358
	All trees	2,321,834	2,541,388	4,863,222	15.217	25.362
South	> 5	25,868,019	29,193,539	55,061,558	9.131	16.079
	< 5	0	7,829,518	7,829,518	1.298	1.298
	All trees	25,868,019	37,023,057	62,891,076	10.429	17.377

[a] Green weight of logging residue assumes a maximum of 60 percent of total residue produced is recoverable.

[b] For harvested trees ≥ 5.0 inches diameter at breast height (d.b.h.), the volume in the bole from a 1-foot stump to a 4-inch top.

[c] For harvested trees ≥ 5.0 inches d.b.h., it is the volume in the portion of the tree above a 4-inch top, and the volume in limbs to a 1-inch end diameter. Also includes total volume (from 1-foot stump to a 1-inch top diameter) of trees < 5.0 inches d b.h.

19

Table A.10—Green weight of softwood recoverable logging residue by State, 1995–2008

State	Size class of harvested trees	Logging residue in harvested trees[a]			Tons per acre	Total tons per acre
		Merchantable[b]	Non-merchantable[c]	Total		
	inches	*green tons*				
Alabama	> 5	977,492	2,992,228	3,969,720	4.744	8.545
	< 5	0	667,179	667,179	0.797	0.797
	All trees	977,492	3,659,407	4,636,899	5.542	9.342
Arkansas	> 5	1,288,806	1,694,334	2,983,140	4.970	8.436
	< 5	0	115,745	115,745	0.193	0.193
	All trees	1,288,806	1,810,079	3,098,885	5.163	8.629
Florida	> 5	700,663	779,742	1,480,405	4.480	8.527
	< 5	0	489,720	489,720	1.482	1.482
	All trees	700,663	1,269,462	1,970,125	5.961	10.009
Georgia	> 5	1,435,193	2,633,966	4,069,159	5.243	9.371
	< 5	0	734,649	734,649	0.947	0.947
	All trees	1,435,193	3,368,615	4,803,808	6.189	10.318
Kentucky	> 5	79,995	40,720	120,715	0.413	0.715
	< 5	0	15,565	15,565	0.053	0.053
	All trees	79,995	56,285	136,280	0.466	0.768
Louisiana	> 5	1,357,848	1,953,327	3,311,175	6.095	10.629
	< 5	0	315,586	315,586	0.581	0.581
	All trees	1,357,848	2,268,913	3,626,761	6.676	11.210
Mississippi	> 5	820,163	809,505	1,629,668	2.810	4.912
	< 5	0	221,949	221,949	0.383	0.383
	All trees	820,163	1,031,454	1,851,617	3.192	5.295
North Carolina	> 5	928,335	1,661,252	2,589,587	6.034	10.366
	< 5	0	200,044	200,044	0.466	0.466
	All trees	928,335	1,861,296	2,789,631	6.586	10.832
Oklahoma (east)	> 5	89,950	78,968	168,918	1.657	3.083
	< 5	0	44,821	44,821	0.440	0.440
	All trees	89,950	123,789	213,739	2.097	3.523
South Carolina	> 5	951,204	2,153,997	3,105,201	7.021	12.401
	< 5	0	410,970	410,970	0.929	0.929
	All trees	951,204	2,564,967	3,516,171	7.950	13.330
Tennessee	> 5	398,959	286,334	685,293	3.012	5.214
	< 5	0	72,394	72,394	0.318	0.318
	All trees	398,959	358,728	757,687	3.330	5.532
Texas (east)	> 5	843,482	1,285,752	2,129,234	3.903	6.911
	< 5	0	308,686	308,686	0.566	0.566
	All trees	843,482	1,594,438	2,437,920	4.469	7.477
Virginia	> 5	668,844	793,853	1,462,697	4.577	8.046
	< 5	0	216,044	216,044	0.676	0.676
	All trees	668,844	1,009,897	1,678,741	5.253	8.722
South	> 5	10,540,934	17,163,978	27,704,912	4.594	8.085
	< 5	0	3,813,352	3,813,352	0.632	0.632
	All trees	10,540,934	20,977,330	31,518,264	5.208	8.717

[a] Green weight of logging residue assumes a maximum of 60 percent of total residue produced is recoverable.

[b] For harvested trees ≥ 5.0 inches diameter at breast height (d.b.h.), the volume in the bole from a 1-foot stump to a 4-inch top.

[c] For harvested trees ≥ 5.0 inches d.b.h., it is the volume in the portion of the tree above a 4-inch top, and the volume in limbs to a 1-inch end diameter. Also includes total volume (from 1-foot stump to a 1-inch top diameter) of trees < 5.0 inches d.b.h.

Table A.11—Green weight of hardwood recoverable logging residue by State, 1995–2008

State	Size class of harvested tree	Recoverable logging residue in harvested trees[a]				
		Merchantable[b]	Non-merchantable[c]	Total	Tons per acre	Total tons per acre
	inches	*green tons*				
Alabama	> 5	1,257,240	1,191,466	2,448,706	2.927	5.557
	< 5	0	866,215	866,215	1.035	1.035
	All trees	1,257,240	2,057,681	3,314,921	3.962	6.592
Arkansas	> 5	1,136,228	1,145,542	2,281,770	3.801	6.582
	< 5	0	224,853	224,853	0.375	0.375
	All trees	1,136,228	1,370,395	2,506,623	4.176	6.957
Florida	> 5	581,615	168,757	750,372	2.271	4.068
	< 5	0	129,669	129,669	0.392	0.392
	All trees	581,615	298,426	880,041	2.663	4.460
Georgia	> 5	1,229,154	854,194	2,083,348	2.684	5.000
	< 5	0	625,039	625,039	0.805	0.805
	All trees	1,229,154	1,479,233	2,708,387	3.490	5.805
Kentucky	> 5	2,181,584	1,701,697	3,883,281	13.291	22.688
	< 5	0	220,414	220,414	0.754	0.754
	All trees	2,181,584	1,922,111	4,103,695	14.046	23.442
Louisiana	> 5	1,585,768	850,726	2,436,494	4.485	8.061
	< 5	0	503,540	503,540	0.927	0.927
	All trees	1,585,768	1,354,266	2,940,034	5.412	8.988
Mississippi	> 5	1,762,504	1,586,179	3,348,683	5.773	10.036
	< 5	0	316,716	316,716	0.546	0.546
	All trees	1,762,504	1,902,895	3,665,399	6.319	10.582
North Carolina	> 5	1,501,270	1,366,937	2,868,207	6.683	11.621
	< 5	0	279,116	279,116	0.650	0.650
	All trees	1,501,270	1,646,053	3,147,323	7.334	12.271
Oklahoma (east)	> 5	169,044	140,105	309,149	3.033	5.436
	< 5	0	57,803	57,803	0.567	0.567
	All trees	169,044	197,908	366,952	3.600	6.003
South Carolina	> 5	579,759	504,964	1,084,723	2.453	4.370
	< 5	0	172,515	172,515	0.390	0.390
	All trees	579,759	677,479	1,257,238	2.843	4.760
Tennessee	> 5	1,057,710	861,832	1,919,542	8.436	14.633
	< 5	0	228,116	228,116	1.002	1.002
	All trees	1,057,710	1,089,948	2,147,658	9.412	15.635
Texas (east)	> 5	632,218	343,770	975,988	1.789	3.167
	< 5	0	174,074	174,074	0.319	0.319
	All trees	632,218	517,844	1,150,062	2.108	3.486
Virginia	> 5	1,652,990	1,313,393	2,966,383	9.281	15.958
	< 5	0	218,098	218,098	0.682	0.682
	All trees	1,652,990	1,531,491	3,184,481	9.963	16.640
South	> 5	15,327,084	12,029,562	27,356,646	4.536	7.994
	< 5	0	4,016,168	4,016,168	0.666	0.666
	All trees	15,327,084	16,045,730	31,372,814	5.179	8.660

[a] Green weight of logging residue assumes a maximum of 60 percent of total residue produced is recoverable.

[b] For harvested trees ≥ 5.0 inches diameter at breast height (d.b.h.), the volume in the bole from a 1-foot stump to a 4-inch top.

[c] For harvested trees ≥ 5.0 inches d.b.h., it is the volume in the portion of the tree above a 4-inch top, and the volume in limbs to a 1-inch end diameter. Also includes total volume (from 1-foot stump to a 1-inch top diameter) of trees < 5.0 inches d.b.h.

Table A.12—Volume of timber removals by removals class, species group, and source, the South, 1995–2008

Removals class and species group	All sources	Source All live removals	Other sources
	thousand cubic feet		
Roundwood products			
Softwood	6,075,131	5,760,646	314,485
Hardwood	2,664,869	2,569,774	95,095
Total	8,740,000	8,330,420	409,580
Logging residues			
Softwood	1,609,952	470,246	1,139,707
Hardwood	1,432,777	657,005	775,772
Total	3,042,729	1,127,251	1,915,478
Other removals			
Softwood	607,966	493,452	114,514
Hardwood	1,219,492	972,868	246,623
Total	1,827,457	1,466,320	361,137
Total removals			
Softwood	8,293,049	6,724,343	1,568,706
Hardwood	5,317,138	4,199,648	1,117,490
Total	13,610,187	10,923,991	2,686,196

Numbers in rows and columns may not sum to totals due to rounding.

Table A.14—Green weight of timber removals by removals class, species group, and source, Alabama, 2001–08

Removals class and species group	All sources	Source All live removals	Other sources
	green tons		
Roundwood products			
Softwood	29,401,533	29,110,611	290,922
Hardwood	10,947,187	10,892,675	54,512
Total	40,348,720	40,003,286	345,434
Logging residues			
Softwood	8,305,899	1,503,834	6,802,065
Hardwood	5,309,707	2,167,655	3,142,052
Total	13,615,606	3,671,489	9,944,117
Other removals			
Softwood	1,359,107	1,103,448	255,659
Hardwood	2,165,411	1,739,621	425,790
Total	3,524,518	2,843,069	681,449
Total removals			
Softwood	39,066,539	31,717,893	7,348,646
Hardwood	18,422,305	14,799,951	3,622,354
Total	57,488,844	46,517,844	10,971,000

Numbers in rows and columns may not sum to totals due to rounding.

Table A.13—Green weight of timber removals by removals class, species group, and source, the South, 1995–2008

Removals class and species group	All sources	Source All live removals	Other sources
	green tons		
Roundwood products			
Softwood	210,823,935	199,909,386	10,914,549
Hardwood	101,752,538	98,118,830	3,633,708
Total	312,576,473	298,028,216	14,548,257
Logging residues			
Softwood	55,873,460	16,318,742	39,554,718
Hardwood	54,729,029	25,085,702	29,643,327
Total	110,602,489	41,404,444	69,198,045
Other removals			
Softwood	21,098,392	17,124,064	3,974,328
Hardwood	46,569,772	37,145,951	9,423,821
Total	67,668,164	54,270,015	13,398,149
Total removals			
Softwood	287,795,787	233,352,192	54,443,595
Hardwood	203,051,339	160,350,483	42,700,856
Total	490,847,126	393,702,675	97,144,451

Numbers in rows and columns may not sum to totals due to rounding.

Table A.15—Green weight of timber removals by removals class, species group, and source, Arkansas, 1996–2004

Removals class and species group	All sources	Source All live removals	Other sources
	green tons		
Roundwood products			
Softwood	16,673,003	16,342,998	330,005
Hardwood	9,290,074	9,142,573	147,501
Total	25,963,077	25,485,571	477,506
Logging residues			
Softwood	5,833,538	1,982,779	3,850,759
Hardwood	4,609,037	1,748,043	2,860,994
Total	10,442,575	3,730,822	6,711,753
Other removals			
Softwood	1,414,757	1,194,921	219,836
Hardwood	3,024,583	2,502,506	522,077
Total	4,439,340	3,697,427	741,913
Total removals			
Softwood	23,921,298	19,520,698	4,400,600
Hardwood	16,923,694	13,393,122	3,530,572
Total	40,844,992	32,913,820	7,931,172

Numbers in rows and columns may not sum to totals due to rounding.

Table A.16—Green weight of timber removals by removals class, species group, and source, Florida, 1995–2007

Removals class and species group	All sources	Source All live removals	Other sources
		green tons	
Roundwood products			
Softwood	16,000,015	14,264,473	1,735,542
Hardwood	2,209,330	1,958,925	250,405
Total	18,209,345	16,223,398	1,985,947
Logging residues			
Softwood	3,155,455	1,045,765	2,109,690
Hardwood	1,450,147	969,358	480,789
Total	4,605,602	2,015,123	2,590,479
Other removals			
Softwood	1,084,070	866,449	217,621
Hardwood	2,122,067	1,698,038	424,029
Total	3,206,137	2,564,487	641,650
Total removals			
Softwood	20,239,540	16,176,687	4,062,853
Hardwood	5,781,544	4,626,321	1,155,223
Total	26,021,084	20,803,008	5,218,076

Numbers in rows and columns may not sum to totals due to rounding.

Table A.18—Green weight of timber removals by removals class, species group, and source, Kentucky, 1988–2007

Removals class and species group	All sources	Source All live removals	Other sources
		green tons	
Roundwood products			
Softwood	392,254	347,459	44,795
Hardwood	7,699,473	7,506,999	192,474
Total	8,091,727	7,854,458	237,269
Logging residues			
Softwood	227,595	129,024	98,571
Hardwood	7,551,788	3,356,282	4,195,506
Total	7,779,383	3,485,306	4,294,077
Other removals			
Softwood	807,085	620,378	186,707
Hardwood	3,681,355	2,622,187	1,059,168
Total	4,488,440	3,242,565	1,245,875
Total removals			
Softwood	1,426,934	1,096,861	330,073
Hardwood	18,932,616	13,485,468	5,447,148
Total	20,359,550	14,582,329	5,777,221

Numbers in rows and columns may not sum to totals due to rounding.

Table A.17—Green weight of timber removals by removals class, species group, and source, Georgia, 1997–2008

Removals class and species group	All sources	Source All live removals	Other sources
		green tons	
Roundwood products			
Softwood	35,711,617	33,407,626	2,303,991
Hardwood	7,932,854	7,930,590	2,264
Total	43,644,471	41,338,216	2,306,255
Logging residues			
Softwood	8,238,131	2,207,990	6,030,141
Hardwood	4,416,106	1,982,506	2,433,600
Total	12,654,237	4,190,496	8,463,741
Other removals			
Softwood	4,160,781	3,371,773	789,008
Hardwood	5,094,139	4,089,305	1,004,834
Total	9,254,920	7,461,078	1,793,842
Total removals			
Softwood	48,110,529	38,987,389	9,123,140
Hardwood	17,443,099	14,002,401	3,440,698
Total	65,553,628	52,989,790	12,563,838

Numbers in rows and columns may not sum to totals due to rounding.

Table A.19—Green weight of timber removals by removals class, species group, and source, Louisiana, 1991–2003

Removals class and species group	All sources	Source All live removals	Other sources
		green tons	
Roundwood products			
Softwood	20,238,351	19,752,955	485,396
Hardwood	8,158,485	7,790,262	368,223
Total	28,396,836	27,543,217	853,619
Logging residues			
Softwood	6,754,216	2,088,997	4,665,219
Hardwood	5,021,268	2,642,947	2,378,321
Total	11,775,484	4,731,944	7,043,540
Other removals			
Softwood	1,438,723	1,159,812	278,911
Hardwood	3,039,341	2,393,768	645,573
Total	4,478,064	3,553,580	924,484
Total removals			
Softwood	28,431,290	23,001,764	5,429,526
Hardwood	16,219,094	12,826,977	3,392,117
Total	44,650,384	35,828,741	8,821,643

Numbers in rows and columns may not sum to totals due to rounding.

Table A.20—Green weight of timber removals by removals class, species group, and source, Mississippi, 1995–2005

Removals class and species group	All sources	Source All live removals	Other sources
		green tons	
Roundwood products			
Softwood	23,544,012	20,381,227	3,162,785
Hardwood	11,739,494	11,359,871	379,623
Total	35,283,506	31,741,098	3,542,408
Logging residues			
Softwood	3,197,478	1,261,790	1,935,688
Hardwood	6,542,457	2,937,506	3,604,951
Total	9,739,935	4,199,296	5,540,639
Other removals			
Softwood	485,317	392,472	92,845
Hardwood	3,485,859	2,954,104	531,755
Total	3,971,176	3,346,576	624,600
Total removals			
Softwood	27,226,807	22,035,489	5,191,318
Hardwood	21,767,810	17,251,481	4,516,329
Total	48,994,617	39,286,970	9,707,647

Numbers in rows and columns may not sum to totals due to rounding.

Table A.22—Green weight of timber removals by removals class, species group, and source, Oklahoma (east), 1994–2008

Removals class and species group	All sources	Source All live removals	Other sources
		green tons	
Roundwood products			
Softwood	2,580,636	2,238,028	342,608
Hardwood	1,612,869	1,532,213	80,656
Total	4,193,505	3,770,241	423,264
Logging residues			
Softwood	349,577	128,501	221,076
Hardwood	642,249	241,492	400,757
Total	991,826	369,993	621,833
Other removals			
Softwood	129,161	104,327	24,834
Hardwood	677,737	533,045	144,692
Total	806,898	637,372	169,526
Total removals			
Softwood	3,059,374	2,470,856	588,518
Hardwood	2,932,855	2,306,750	626,105
Total	5,992,229	4,777,606	1,214,623

Numbers in rows and columns may not sum to totals due to rounding.

Table A.21—Green weight of timber removals by removals class, species group, and source, North Carolina, 2002–07

Removals class and species group	All sources	Source All live removals	Other sources
		green tons	
Roundwood products			
Softwood	17,652,932	17,198,535	454,397
Hardwood	11,700,513	11,452,451	248,062
Total	29,353,445	28,650,986	702,459
Logging residues			
Softwood	5,157,168	1,428,208	3,728,960
Hardwood	5,688,451	2,502,117	3,186,334
Total	10,845,619	3,930,325	6,915,294
Other removals			
Softwood	2,752,340	2,247,569	504,771
Hardwood	7,359,776	5,906,177	1,453,599
Total	10,112,116	8,153,746	1,958,370
Total removals			
Softwood	25,562,440	20,874,312	4,688,128
Hardwood	24,748,740	19,860,745	4,887,995
Total	50,311,180	40,735,057	9,576,123

Numbers in rows and columns may not sum to totals due to rounding.

Table A.23—Green weight of timber removals by removals class, species group, and source, South Carolina, 2001–07

Removals class and species group	All sources	Source All live removals	Other sources
		green tons	
Roundwood products			
Softwood	18,279,275	18,242,804	36,471
Hardwood	4,865,394	4,726,506	138,888
Total	23,144,669	22,969,310	175,359
Logging residues			
Softwood	6,172,529	1,585,340	4,587,189
Hardwood	2,189,695	966,265	1,223,430
Total	8,362,224	2,551,605	5,810,619
Other removals			
Softwood	2,807,105	2,275,659	531,446
Hardwood	2,459,822	1,984,863	474,959
Total	5,266,927	4,260,522	1,006,405
Total removals			
Softwood	27,258,909	22,103,803	5,155,106
Hardwood	9,514,911	7,677,634	1,837,277
Total	36,773,820	29,781,437	6,992,383

Numbers in rows and columns may not sum to totals due to rounding.

Table A.24—Green weight of timber removals by removals class, species group, and source, Tennessee, 1999–2007

Removals class and species group	All sources	Source All live removals	Other sources
		green tons	
Roundwood products			
Softwood	2,988,488	2,889,614	98,874
Hardwood	10,137,293	9,324,941	812,352
Total	13,125,781	12,214,555	911,226
Logging residues			
Softwood	1,320,771	613,783	706,988
Hardwood	3,771,783	1,762,850	2,008,933
Total	5,092,554	2,376,633	2,715,921
Other removals			
Softwood	725,878	590,139	135,739
Hardwood	3,847,806	3,065,547	782,259
Total	4,573,684	3,655,686	917,998
Total removals			
Softwood	5,035,137	4,093,536	941,601
Hardwood	17,756,882	14,153,338	3,603,544
Total	22,792,019	18,246,874	4,545,145

Numbers in rows and columns may not sum to totals due to rounding.

Table A.26—Green weight of timber removals by removals class, species group, and source, Virginia, 2002–07

Removals class and species group	All sources	Source All live removals	Other sources
		green tons	
Roundwood products			
Softwood	8,963,294	8,574,166	389,128
Hardwood	10,145,675	9,841,310	304,365
Total	19,108,969	18,415,476	693,493
Logging residues			
Softwood	2,884,395	1,045,068	1,839,327
Hardwood	5,650,472	2,754,984	2,895,488
Total	8,534,867	3,800,052	4,734,815
Other removals			
Softwood	2,500,438	2,030,139	470,299
Hardwood	7,572,833	6,038,800	1,534,033
Total	10,073,271	8,068,939	2,004,332
Total removals			
Softwood	14,348,127	11,649,373	2,698,754
Hardwood	23,368,980	18,635,094	4,733,886
Total	37,717,107	30,284,467	7,432,640

Numbers in rows and columns may not sum to totals due to rounding.

Table A.25—Green weight of timber removals by removals class, species group, and source, Texas (east), 2003–07

Removals class and species group	All sources	Source All live removals	Other sources
		green tons	
Roundwood products			
Softwood	18,398,526	17,158,891	1,239,635
Hardwood	5,313,899	4,659,516	654,383
Total	23,712,425	21,818,407	1,894,018
Logging residues			
Softwood	4,276,702	1,297,665	2,979,037
Hardwood	1,885,869	1,053,697	832,172
Total	6,162,571	2,351,362	3,811,209
Other removals			
Softwood	1,433,631	1,166,977	266,654
Hardwood	2,039,043	1,617,990	421,053
Total	3,472,674	2,784,967	687,707
Total removals			
Softwood	24,108,859	19,623,533	4,485,326
Hardwood	9,238,811	7,331,203	1,907,608
Total	33,347,670	26,954,736	6,392,934

Numbers in rows and columns may not sum to totals due to rounding.